YOU, LITTLE GIRL!

LABANNYA ROY

Made with ❤ on the Notion Press Platform
www.notionpress.com

For

Maa and Baba,

Indrajit, Prithwijit

My son Yudhajit

This work is dedicated with profound appreciation and admiration
to all the resilient young girls navigating betrayals and solitude.
May it serve as, a beacon of hope and resilience to all who
encounter its pages.

**When I decided to write my first book, I told him that his
name would be in it.
So, this book is for you as well, Suddhasatta.**

Contents

Contents

Preface

I've always dreamed of writing a book since I was a child. This desire intensified in 2012, the year a significant event in my life made this dream even more fervent. That year, something happened that ignited an unstoppable urge to put my thoughts and feelings into words. So, I began writing, no matter how small or big the pieces were, constantly telling myself that one day I would share my innermost thoughts with the world.

When my father passed away, I was quite young; but old enough to understand everything. During his last rites, I remained strong, telling myself that I needed to be resilient for the sake of my mother and younger brother.

After my father's departure, someone came into my life who became very close to me. Over the next six years, we shared many experiences, both good and bad. He promised me that he would never leave, but sometimes, life doesn't allow us to hold on to the ones we love. Eventually, we parted ways. I don't blame him, but I was devastated and cried a lot. It feels like 14 years might not be enough to forget a love that lasted six years. However, I'm grateful to God for bringing him into my life and for the love we shared. Today, I am with someone who loves me dearly.

Acknowledgements

The fruition of this imaginative endeavour has been made possible through the gracious support and assistance of numerous individuals, to whom I owe profound gratitude.

First and foremost, I extend my heartfelt appreciation to the divine for the wisdom bestowed upon me, the fortitude granted, and the tranquil peace of mind that enabled me to bring this book to fruition.

I am deeply indebted to my parents for their unwavering encouragement, which served as a beacon guiding me through the completion of this book. To my mother, **Kaberi Roy**, and my father, **Lt. Pradip Kumar Roy**, your constant presence during challenging times and your unwavering belief in me inspired me to strive for excellence.

To my beloved and supportive husband, **Prithwijit De**, your counsel and encouragement propelled me forward urging me to persevere until the completion of this endeavour.

My gratitude extends to my cherished son, **Yudhajit De**, and my dear little brother, **Indrajit Roy**, their boundless love and presence have been a constant source of joy and inspiration.

Special appreciation is reserved for my best friend, **Sutapa Nath**, whose unwavering belief in my abilities and staunch disapproval of any doubts spurred me on. My friend **Swarnavo Ghosh**, your willingness to read and provide feedback on my work before submission was invaluable.

ACKNOWLEDGEMENTS

Lastly, I am immensely grateful to all my readers and to each & every individual who has left an indelible mark on my life, reminding me of the richness of human connection and the power of collective memory.

• x •

Prologue

This phrase resonates deeply with many of us. We've all encountered it at some point in our lives, often when we've been let down by someone we trusted. For me, this phrase came from the lips of someone I loved, someone who promised to stand by me forever, especially when I needed him the most. Yet, when the time came when I was at my most vulnerable after losing my father, he chose to leave. He walked away for his happiness, and while I understand his choice, his parting words—"Promises are meant to be broken"—left a scar that I carry with me to this day.

It was in this period of profound heartbreak that I began to write. What you're about to read isn't just a collection of poems; it's a raw and honest outpouring of my emotions. Each word has been penned with teary eyes and a heavy heart. Initially, I never intended to share these writings with anyone. I feared ridicule and judgment. The thought of exposing my innermost feelings to the world was terrifying. It's not easy to become an open book, to step out of one's shell and lay bare one's soul. But here I am, taking that leap of faith, sharing this introduction and the collection that follows with you.

I hope that these words will resonate with others who are going through their own struggles. I know there are many out there, especially young women, who are facing difficulties and seeking peace of mind, yet feeling as if they are coming up empty-handed. To you, I say: I understand. I've been in that dark place, and I know how it feels.

The journey often starts with a single, seemingly simple word: 'Promise.'

I won't ask you to stop feeling hurt because heartbreak is a heavy burden. It makes you question everything, including yourself. But I do urge you to hold on. Be brave and keep faith in yourself and most importantly in God. Remember, life tests those who are willing to stand up and fight back.

So, with that said, I present to you this collection of my feelings, my heartbreaks, and my hopes. I offer these words to you, hoping they bring you some solace and perhaps a bit of understanding. Whether you love, hate, or feel indifferent towards what I've written, I hope you find a piece of your own journey reflected here.

Wishing you happiness and strength,
Labannya Roy

1. yours, 'Buru'

In a distant land, you wandered away,
Beyond my reach, where I cannot sway.
The day you departed, my soul did stray,
And within, a part of me did decay.
People gathered, their eyes swollen with tears,
In our abode, grief echoed for years.
I prayed to the heavens, amidst all my fears,
For peace to embrace you, beyond mortal spheres.
In the shadows, I've wandered alone,
In the darkest hours, where no solace is shown.
Yet, in the distance, your presence is known,
Guiding me silently, though you're far from home.
Countless oceans, I've shed in despair,
Your absence is a burden, too heavy to bear.
Yet, amidst the anguish, a whisper of prayer,
For strength to endure, in the void we share.
Years have passed since you slipped away,
Each moment, I yearn for your comforting sway.
Though life unfolds, in its relentless sway,
My heart remains tethered, where you forever stay.
I hold onto hope, in the depths of my soul,
That someday, miraculously, our paths may unfold.
Until then, in dreams, my longing will enrol,

In your presence, my solace, I'll forever extol.

So I'll wait in the shadows, with bated breath,

For the day when reunion triumphs over death.

Till then, in dreams, where there's no parting's wrath,

You'll be my peace, lighting love's eternal path.

2. Quotes on Me

When life bestows lemons upon your path,
And the recipe for lemonade eludes your grasp,
Fear not the sour twist of fate's design,
For within the bitter, sweetness, you'll find.
In the depths of uncertainty, seeds of hope are sown,
With patience and courage, a new path is shown.
Embrace the challenge, let resilience bloom,
From life's tart lemons, your own nectar you'll consume.

3. She's One of Us

She is a girl with black and white,
Strings entwined with emotions and vows,
Hard to fathom what's within her mind's sight,
Never yielding, never bowing, never drowse.
Love, a fleeting word she claims her own,
Hatred she shuns, anger she steers,
Logic her guide, in realms unknown,
Beautiful, she is, devoid of fears.
Compassion her beacon, pure yet fierce,
Power within, yet stirred by plight,
Passionate whispers, her essence pierce,
In her depths, a silent fight.
Trust her when she pleads for aid,
Do not dismiss her pleas as mere deceive,
Issues she simplifies, in truth, swayed,
Yet her silent struggles, we must perceive.
Amazing, when she dares to dream,
God, heal her scars, her wounds unbind,
Bless her, save her, in your gleam,
For she's your child, in spirit entwined.
Through tempests, she'll navigate and soar,
Tides will ebb, calm will unfold,
Patience grant her, let not her spirit sore,

In solitude's battle, let her brave heart hold.

Strength endows her, grants her life's embrace,

Shield her from cowards, who with poison plots,

She cries for aid, lost in life's maze,

Drowning deep, yet pleading to be sought.

Help her, O Lord! Let her light shine,

For she's one of us, in humanity's grace divine.

4. Glittering Eyes

Sparkling lights in the vast abyss,
Blinking like lightning bugs' soft kiss.
A distant moon with all her flaws,
Shining through both day and night's applause.
Oh Father, Oh Friend, in you we confide,
Blame not the past, let love be our guide.
Promise of solace, promise of light,
Together we'll weather the darkest of night.
Oh Mother, Oh Brother, and lovers divine,
May blessings rain upon you, like sweet wine.
Dreaming of love, in its purest form,
Exploring the beauty, weathering the storm.
Imagining dragons with flames reaching high,
Posters on walls, where dreams amplify.
Blurry the lines as morning light breaks,
Embrace the unknown, whatever it takes.
Drink from the cup of life's sweet embrace,
Dream anew, in this boundless space.

5. A Wrinkle in Time

I won't blame my past lovers for break-ups,
Instead, I'm grateful they showed me the way,
Each parting taught me lessons I treasure,
Lessons my parents and teachers couldn't convey.
From their selfishness, I learned selflessness,
And to find joy in life's simple embrace,
Their rudeness taught me kindness,
And the importance of grace.
Their carelessness taught me to cherish time,
And to embrace love with all my might,
Being taken for granted taught me boundaries,
And the courage to stand up for what's right.
Through them, I discovered my bravery,
And how to navigate emotions with care,
Now, I'm ready to move forward,
With a heart that's more aware.
I won't dwell on the past, for life's too short,
To waste on regrets and pain,
Instead, I'll treasure each moment,
And dance in the sunshine and rain.
For in every wrinkle of time,
There lies a lesson, a chance to grow,
So, let's embrace each moment,

And let our true selves show.
Let's cherish the journey, the highs and lows,
For who knows what tomorrow may bring,
But with these lessons etched in our souls,
We'll face whatever life may sling.

6. Dreams

In shadows deep, where fears abide,

Incubus, thy presence hide,

For in the recess of my soul's domain,

I'll not yield to thy dark refrain.

With every breath, I'll fortify,

My spirit's fortress, strong and high,

And though doubts may dance in twilight's glow,

I'll steer my course where dreams do flow.

The future waits with bated breath,

A tale unwritten, life's dance and death,

Yet in this moment, we find our power,

To seize the day, our finest hour.

So let us stand hand in hand

Against the tides, against the sand,

And let our dreams take flight and soar,

To distant shores, forever-more.

For in this journey, side by side,

We'll brave the storms, with hearts untied,

And though the past may haunt our way,

We'll face it boldly, come what may.

So, Incubus, with all thy might

Seek not to dim my guiding light,

For in my dreams, I shall prevail,

And turn the darkness into a fairytale.

7. Escapes Reality

Reading is what she enjoys the most,
Nothing gives her chills, raising goosebumps like a ghost.
Traveling far away to fantasy lands,
Feeling the characters deep within her hands.
Touching emotions with her fingertips,
Each story, a journey that beautifully grips.
Words dance, playing with our imaginations,
In the tangled mess of life's complications.
Reading makes her feel truly alive,
While other things leave her sad and deprived.
In moments of heartbreak and lonely times,
She escapes reality through prose and rhymes.
So, she delves into pages, seeking solace and flight,
In the realm of books, where worlds take flight.
Where every story, though not quite real,
Has the power to heal and make her feel.

8. What If

What if I were to vanish from the street
You walk behind, without a trace or sound?
(Imagine you're strolling down a quiet street, and suddenly, the person ahead of you disappears into thin air. There's no noise, no sign of where they went, just an empty path ahead)
What if I became a bird and soared high
With wings outstretched, embracing the sky?
(Picture me transforming into a bird. I spread my wings wide and lifted off the ground, flying high above. The wind carries me, and I feel free, touching the clouds and seeing the world below)
What if I transformed into a child once more
With a lollipop in hand, innocence in store?
(Think of me turning back into a little child, holding a colourful lollipop. I'm filled with pure joy and innocence, just like in those carefree days of childhood)
What if my nightmares, just for one night's gleam
Turned into dreams, as sweet as a moonbeam?
(Imagine that, for one special night, all my scary nightmares disappear. In their place, I have the most beautiful dreams, soft and sweet like the gentle light of the moon)
What if I could return to that little girl's embrace
Living in a world where joy finds its place?

(Envision me going back to a time when I was a small child, safe in my mother's arms. In that world, happiness is all around, and everything feels just right)

9. Misery

I don't like mornings
They remind me of new beginnings,
Yet people say mornings are good,
As we move forward in life, as we should.
I don't like nights
They remind me of partial ends,
Forced to accept what fate sends.
I don't enjoy staying wide awake,
Just to ponder and panic, for goodness' sake.
But one thing I do savour,
Is the idea of sound sleep, in my behaviour?
Isn't that something we all yearn for,
Once in a while, to seek a tranquil shore?

10. She is

She endured endless pain,
amidst shattered love and broken chains,
each scar a reminder, etched in vain,
reflected in the mirror's disdain.
Those she cherished, all departed,
leaving behind memories, cold-hearted,
silently whispering, as they parted,
abandoning her, world-weary and disheartened.
She vowed no more love to give,
no more hearts to sieve,
to marry the one who'd truly live,
in her love, faithfully and forgive.
Though it would rend her soul apart,
she'd brave the pain, with a steadfast heart,
calculating the cost, she'd impart,
for a love that wouldn't depart.
Gradually, she became a warrior fair,
mending her spirit with tender care,
from the ashes, she rose, aware,
a princess of resilience, beyond compare.

11. Hopelessness

She bore so much pain,
beyond all comprehension,
Yet, she carried on,
with love as her mission.
She gave up so many,
for those she held dear,
Yet, in her sacrifice,
no hint of fear.
Through trials and tests,
lessons she did learn,
Now, she imparts wisdom,
for others to discern.
Battling her demons,
with a smile so bright,
In her darkest moments,
she found her light.
Lost in sorrow's grip,
yet never to submit,
For in her journey,
hope she'll permit.
With each passing day,
she strives to impart,
A glimmer of hope,

to each weary heart.

12. Pain

Have you ever wondered what pain smells like?
To me, it's like gasping for air,
Struggling to breathe amidst toxicity,
Betrayed by those around you,
Alone in your suffocating despair.
Pain smells like 'Nothingness',
Like the scent of 'Death',
A constant companion in shame and regret,
It lingers day and night, relentless.
It spreads like a virus,
Corrupting everything it touches,
A disease of the soul,
That you can't outrun or hide from.
Pain smells like everything
We fear to confront in life.
It's a cruel reality,
Yet, a reminder that we're alive.
They say, 'No Pain, No Gain',
A truth I've come to embrace.
For in feeling pain, in smelling pain,
We affirm our existence in this mortal race.
Sometimes pain smells like helium,
Floating like balloons in the sky,

Fragile and ready to burst,

Yet soaring, defying the lows.

But pain is more than words can convey,

It's the silence in between,

The loneliness in a crowd,

A deep slumber from which we may never awake.

So let pain be our reminder,

That we're still among the living,

For the day it no longer matters,

Is the day we cease to be, unforgiving.

13. Sculpture's Divinity

In ancient times of mythic lore,
On Olympus' peak, the gods did soar.
Zeus, with lightning in his hand,
Ruled over both sea and land.
Hera, with her marriage's sway,
Guided lovers on their way.
Poseidon, mighty in his might,
Commanded oceans, dark as night.
Demeter, with her fields so vast,
Ensured each harvest came to pass.
Ares, fierce in battle's dance,
Led armies with a warrior's stance.
Athena, wise with eyes so keen,
Guarded olive groves serene.
Apollo, with his lyre's song,
Inspired art and righted wrong.
Artemis, with bow in hand,
Hunted prey across the land.
Hephaestus, in his fiery forge,
Crafted wonders to emerge.
Aphrodite, with beauty's grace,
Brought love's blush to every face.
Hermes, fleet of foot and mind,

Linked mortals to the divine.

Dionysus, with wine's sweet taste,

Brought joy to every feast.

Hades, ruler of the shades,

Guided souls through death's dark glades.

Hypnos, gentle in his sleep,

Watched o'er dreams both wide and deep.

Nike, with victory's gleaming light,

Urged champions to take flight.

Janus, with his gates of old,

Marked beginnings, endings told.

Nemesis, with her balancing hand,

Restored justice across the land.

Iris, with her rainbow's hue,

Brought messages both false and true.

Hecate, in the shadows' gleam,

Guided magic as in a dream.

Tychy, with fortune's fickle game,

Brought both wealth and fleeting fame.

Through time's passage, myths remain,

Echoes of an ancient reign.

Sculptors' hands, like poets' verse,

Capture gods in stone's converse.

Though museums hold their silent art,

Their stories still stir mortal hearts.

For in each figure, chiselled true,

Lies the essence of what we knew.

So let the tales of old inspire,

And keep the flame of myth afire.

In books we read, in knowledge seek,

But deeper truths may yet lie bleak.

For sculptures speak in silent tongues,

Of gods and mortals, old and young.

So let us honour, let us cherish,

The myths that in our hearts still flourish.

For in their tales, we find our own,

A legacy is forever known.

"In the ancient city of Athens, nestled among the olive groves and marble columns, there stood a grand museum, dedicated to the Gods of old. Within its halls, sculptures of mythic deities adorned every corner. Each one was crafted with such skill and artistry, that they seemed to come alive with tales, of their own.

Among the visitors to this museum was a young girl named Callista. With wide eyes and a heart full of wonder, she wandered through the galleries, marvelling at the lifelike forms of Zeus, Hera, and the other gods and goddesses of Mount Olympus.

As she gazed upon the sculptures, Callista felt a strange sensation, as if the stone figures were whispering secrets to her. She reached out to touch the cold marble of Athena's statue, and suddenly, she was transported back in time to ancient Greece.

In this mythical realm Callista found herself amid a great feast on Olympus. The gods and goddesses laughed and danced, their voices echoing through the halls of the divine palace. Zeus, with his lightning bolt in hand: presided over the festivities, while Hera, radiant in her regal gown, smiled upon the revelry.

Callista watched in awe as Poseidon stirred the seas with a wave of his trident, and Demeter blessed the fields with bountiful harvests. Ares, clashed his sword in battle, while Athena, wise and serene, looked on with a knowing gaze.

As the night wore on, Callista found herself drawn to the graceful figure of Artemis, the goddess of the hunt. Together, they roamed through moonlit forests, hunting prey beneath the starry sky.

But soon, it was time for Callista to return to the present day. With a heavy heart, she bid farewell to the gods and goddesses of Olympus, knowing that their world would forever remain beyond her reach.

Back in the museum, Callista looked upon the sculptures

with newfound reverence. Though; they were made of stone, they held within them the essence of a bygone era- a time when gods walked among mortals and magic filled the air. And as she left the museum behind, Callista carried with her the memories, of her journey into mythic lore, knowing that the tales of the gods would forever inspire her heart and soul."

14. Pretending

Let's pretend like nothing's amiss,
I'll hide my tears with a blissful kiss.
Pretend it doesn't weigh heavy on your mind,
I'll mask my worries, and leave them behind.
If whispers carry tales of woe,
I'll feign deafness, let them go.
Pretend you're strong, a fighter true,
I'll don my armour, and stand with you.
A smile, bright and bold, I'll wear,
Though inside, doubts may tear.
Haters may sneer, but we'll rise above,
In our pretence, find strength and love.
Hide the cracks, don't let them see,
Pretend with me, we'll dance carefree.
In this charade, we'll find our way,
Pretending everything's okay.

15. Random

Never have I ever dreamt of you,
Yet, if fate permits, I'd cherish the view,
Forgiveness and love, my constant plea,
Life's gift, devoid of sin, for me to see.
What more could one desire, I implore,
No room for error just, farewells in-store,
If ever I glimpse you with eyes divine,
I'll cling to you, my saviour, forever thine.
In the dance of time, if our paths align,
I'll hold you close, our souls entwined,
For you are my beacon, my guiding light,
In your embrace, all wrongs set right.
So, if destiny deems our hearts to meet,
I'll never let go, my devotion complete,
You, my salvation, in every hue,
In this vast world, my love, it's you.

16. Monster In Us

The monster within is insatiable,
incessantly tearing me apart,
and I'm helpless to resist,
except to ingest the sickness
that's already infected my soul.
I'll forever rely on a substance
to keep me breathing.
Sobriety births deafening screams
in the pit of my being,
yet this vice hushes them,
if only for a fleeting moment.
Children fear monsters beneath their beds,
but as we age,
we realize they reside within us,
waiting to be, acknowledged.
Sometimes, we must delve
deeper and deeper
into our twisted souls.

17. Writing Makes Me Happier

I don't write for others,

I write for myself,

For my happiness,

In this moment of quiet,

I reflect on my unfinished business.

A piece of me always seeks

Peace, love, solace,

Yet they elude my grasp,

Hidden away in shadows.

I don't act in times of normalcy,

But when silence reigns,

I speak the truth, even if it stings,

For in honesty, there is clarity.

Life's brevity warns against regret,

Urging us to choose wisely,

To trust oneself is to be a beacon,

Guiding both self and loved ones.

Before leaping to the other side,

Pause and ponder,

For the bridge may crumble,

And wounds may deepen,

In the pursuit of causing harm.

18. Sanity

In the ethereal embrace of your touch,
the heavens sigh with seven shadows,
each a whispered secret of beauty's allure.
Yet beneath the surface, flaws adorn
the canvas of your soul,
each imperfection, a testament
to the shards you've gathered,
vowing never to scatter again.
Decency, a phantom dance
in the minds of mortals,
yet it eludes grasp like wisps of smoke,
leaving nought but tales of hardship
and fleeting counsel, a tapestry of wisdom.
Clever, you are, to arrange
the chaos of existence
into a symphony of meaning,
each discordant note finding its harmony.
And as your Holy Grail grazes my skin,
I am anointed with the grace of your touch,
blessed by the alchemy of our union.

19. Oh Love

Nothing is impossible,
Now, I stand on my own,
Rebuilding amidst the unknown,
In every soul, in every bone.
From the darkest hour,
The devil of my past,
Tested me with its power,
But I rose steadfast.
They don't comprehend,
The depths of my hue,
Like you, my friend,
Who sees me as true?
Blowing candles, back to work,
With newfound resolve,
In every challenge, I lurk,
Determined to evolve.
I get ready, adorned with grace,
For the journey, undefined,
In every step, I embrace,
My essence is refined.
It matters not if I'm deemed enough,
For the paths untrodden,
For I am young, love, and tough,

In myself, I've found solace, unbidden.

Oh Love, there's no more confusion,

Just the bliss of self-discovery,

In this wild dance of illusion,

I revel in love, unconditionally.

20. Beautiful Yesterday

Now and then, memories flood my mind,
Of days when we were intertwined,
You once said you felt joy to die,
But in your presence, I felt a lonely sigh.
A love that stings, aches, and twists,
Leaves behind scars that persist,
Addicted to a sorrow so deep,
Resigned to the end, where tears seep.
You said we'd still be friends, but I'm glad it's done,
No longer tethered, our ties undone,
You didn't have to vanish like a ghost,
Leaving me to wander, lost.
You didn't need to cut me off so clean,
Like a scene erased, never to be seen,
Treating me like a stranger, cold and rough,
Now just a memory, somebody that I used to love.
Now I ponder the times you caused me pain,
Yet made me believe I was to blame,
I refuse to dwell in that web of lies,
Parsing words, deciphering alibis.
You claimed you could move on, let it flow,
But I see you trapped, unable to let go,
Hanging onto fragments of the past,

A prisoner of memories that forever last.

21. Where Rainbow Ends

Life's not just bleak, it's a canvas to seek,
In each twist and turn, there's meaning to peek.
Solving the riddle, on paths we tread,
Leads to joy where shadows, once spread.
Through tunnels dark, and trials severe,
We push through when hope's not near.
Though edges tempt, you to let go and fall,
We rise again, answering life's call.
In this strange dance, of rain and shine,
We find our rhythm, in the grand design.
For where the rainbow bends, our hearts transcend,
To the peace we seek, where dreams ascend.

22. Dolly

In those quiet moments, when the world fades away,

You'll remember my words, as clear as day.

In laughter and sorrow, you found your game,

But in my absence, will it ever be the same?

For whom will your jests be, and who will shed those tears?

In my absence, would you be able to face your fears?

No, you'll not find another, so unique, so dear,

A doll like me, forever near.

Today, I cry for what we had,

Tomorrow, it will be your heart feeling sad.

Silent tears, hidden from sight,

In the darkness of your quiet night,

You'll want to scream, break the chains,

But I'll be up there, watching, beyond earthly pains,

Just like the stars gaze upon me now,

I'll see your sorrow, though you won't know how.

For I am but human, and humans do cry,

Missing the moments that passed us by.

Can you give me back those lost days,

The cherished memories, the time that sways?

Give me back those eight years we spent,

I know you can't, but my heart's lament,

Spoke of the wish to live again,

Can I? Will I? It's all in vain.
Yet, here I've poured my soul in verse,
The rest, we'll save for the universe,
Another time, another day,
When words are all that's left to say.

23. I am

Who are you?
To judge,
To teach,
To manipulate,
To disown,
Nobody.
You're more than perceived,
Greater than mere existence,
Deserving beyond possessions,
You're you.
Purely you.
You're the essence of your best self.
Live it.
Believe it.
Trust, your instincts.
Never rue decisions made,
Each one is a lesson, a guide,
For in every choice lies growth.
Remember, decisions crafted
For the pursuit of your joy,
Are never in vain.

24. Love Is Love

Sometimes we falter in life's grand ballet,
Love becomes the scapegoat in dismay,
Blaming its essence for our own mistakes,
Yet love's beauty in our hearts still awakes.
Love, a melody both serene and sweet,
Yet it's the storm where our paths may meet,
We label it, define it, try to contain,
But love defies logic, and knows no domain.
Love, neither all nor nought, but a dance,
In its simplicity, we find our chance,
To let it be, unburdened by our needs,
For love's true essence, in freedom, it leads.
So let love be, a whisper in the breeze,
L. O. V. E., a simple, gentle tease,
In its four letters, a world so vast,
And in its mystery, we find peace at last.

25. Jack N Rose

Childhood days, oh so sweet,
When dreams danced at our feet.
Teachers asked, with eyes so bright,
"What will you be?" in the morning light.
Some said astronauts, to touch the stars,
Others, doctors healing scars.
But I, in whispers soft and low,
Dreamt of being art's own glow.
To be a model, not for fame,
But for the canvas, where dreams became.
Paint me with colours, bold and true,
Touch me gently, make me new.
Just like Jack, with Rose so fair,
In Titanic's tale, beyond compare.
Let the brush strokes tell our story,
In art's embrace, we'll find our glory.

26. Journey of Reflections

As I stroll along the bustling streets, adorned with luxurious cars and beautifully dressed people, it's hard not to notice the stark contrast of lifestyles. It's almost as if everyone is in a race, but for what? Material possessions seem to be the measure of success, but is that really where happiness lies?

As I ponder these thoughts, my stomach grumbles, reminding me of my empty pockets. The desire for something to eat tugs at my heart, yet the reality of not having, enough money weighs heavily on my mind. I glance at the road ahead, wondering how long I'll have to wear these worn-out half-pants. Just make ends meet.

Money... where does one find it? It seems, to flow effortlessly into the hands of those walking past me. They seem like good people, capable of giving, but will they? Maybe... let's see.

As I continue my journey, thoughts of indulging in warm, sweet jalebis or perhaps some biscuits, or even better yet, ice cream, dance in my mind. The idea of, treating myself to such delights brings a smile to my face. But alas, there's no money for such luxuries.

"No one gives anything for free, do they?" I wonder aloud, feeling the weight of reality pressing down on me.

Suddenly, a voice breaks through my reverie. A stranger, a woman, hands me some money. My heart leaps with gratitude as I accept her kindness. It's a moment of pure joy, a glimmer of hope amid struggle.

But as I turn to leave, I hear another voice behind me. A man, perhaps less fortunate than myself, asks for help. Without hesitation, I pass on some of the money, I've just received. The cycle continues, a chain of giving and receiving, each act a reminder of the interconnectedness of humanity.

In that moment, amidst the chaos of the city streets, I find peace. For it's not the material wealth that defines us, but the compassion and kindness we show to one another. And as I walk away, I carry with me the profound lesson that true richness lies not in what we possess, but in how we choose to share our blessings with others.

27. Decision Is Yours

You embarked on a journey years ago,
Now, you walk alone, with your flow.
Only you hold the map to your rest,
And where to draw the line, you know best.

Decisions lie solely in your hands,
As you search for answers across lands.
Questions abound, seeking to find,
The wisdom and truth to ease your mind.

You have travelled through valleys deep and wide,
Climbed mountains with strength as your guide.
Through forests, dense and deserts dry
Under the vast and endless sky.

Each step you take, each path you choose,
Leads you to places, where you win or lose.
But every moment, whether bright or grey,
Shapes your soul, in a unique way.

In the quiet of the night, you often ponder,
About the journey and its endless wonder.
The stars above seem to understand,
The dreams and hopes you have at hand.

There are times you feel weary and worn,
From the trials faced and the burdens borne.
But in your heart, there's a light that glows,
A reminder of why this path you chose.

You meet strangers along the way,
Some who help, some who stray.
Each encounter leaves a mark,
A lesson learned a spark in the dark.

You have known joy and felt despair,
Held, onto faith and breathed in the air.
Of new beginnings and fresh starts,
Healing old wounds and mending hearts.

As days turn to months and months to years,
You find strength in overcoming fears.
The road is long, but you are strong,

With a spirit that has known where it belongs.

Sometimes, you stop to rest and reflect,
On all the moments, both perfect and wrecked.
The laughter shared, the tears that fell,
The stories that you now can tell.

And though the end is not yet near,
You hold onto dreams, precious and dear.
For every journey must come to an end,
But until then, your heart will mend.

With courage as your steadfast friend,
You continue, around each bend.
Knowing well that life's true quest,
Is not the end but every test.

So walk on, traveller, with head held high,
Beneath the sun and moonlit sky.
For you are the author of your tale,
A testament, to how dreams prevail.

28. Hidden Away

The heart wanders in the depths of sorrow,
seeking purpose amidst the unknown expanse,
feeling adrift and hollow.
Fragmented by the trials of life,
it struggles to forge ahead,
its dreams and aspirations shattered,
obscured in the shadows of uncertainty.
Once held dear,
trust now seems as futile as truth and falsehood
blend into a perplexing amalgam,
challenging discernment.
Yet, amid the turmoil,
a subtle yearning stirs within,
prompting contemplation on the nature of resilience.
Can we endure the pain, deceit, and tears,
only to rise once more, forever changed?
Perhaps, the heart muses,
concealing desires shields them from further anguish,
sparing it from the vulnerability of loss.
In embracing this guarded stance,
the heart seeks solace,
finding refuge in its modest grievances,
preserving its purity amidst the chaos of existence.

29. Living Again

My sadness no longer hinges on you,
Yet my joy still finds solace in your hue.
Thus, I embrace life anew,
In a realm of colours, fresh and true.
With every dawn, a chance to grow,
To let my spirit freely flow.
In the embrace of joy, I find,
A peace that soothes my troubled mind.
Though shadows linger from the past,
I step forward, free at last.
For in this journey, I've found my voice,
And in my light, I rejoice.
The days of sorrow now seem far,
Like distant memories, fading scars.
I walk the path with a hopeful heart,
For every end, a new start.
In the morning sun, I see
A world of endless possibility.
The sky, a canvas, vast and wide,
With every shade of life inside.
Gone are the days of endless nights
Replaced by dreams, bathed in light.
Each step I take, a dance, a song,

A melody where I belong.

The whisper of the wind, the rustle of the leaves,

They speak of change, of hopes, of dreams.

And in their gentle, soothing sound,

A sense of calm is always found.

With friends beside me, old and new,

We share the laughter, joys, and hues.

Together we face the future's call,

With courage and love, we stand tall.

I cherish moments, big and small,

In each one, I find my all.

For life's journey, rich and sweet,

With every challenge, a chance to meet.

The stars at night, they guide my way,

Reminding me of brighter days.

And in their twinkle, soft and pure,

I find hope that will endure.

So here I stand, with open arms,

Embracing life, its joys, its charms.

For every tear, there's a smile,

And every step, a worthwhile mile.

The lessons learned; the love I've gained,

Have shaped the person I've remained.

And though the past has left its mark,

It's lit the flame within the dark.

I cherish the love, the pain, the fear,

For they have brought me standing here.
And with a heart, resilient, strong,
I sing anew my life's own song.

So as I journey down this road,
I carry light, a brighter load.
For in the end, it's clear to see,
The power of hope, of dreams set free.

Each morning brings a brand-new start,
A chance to heal a mending heart.
With eyes that see the world anew,
In every colour, bright and true.

And though the shadows sometimes fall,
I stand up straight, I stand up tall.
For in my heart, I've found the key,
To live life, abundantly free.

30. Heartbreak's Lesson

Promises break,
Hearts ache,
But still, we hold on.
Tears may fall,
Yet through it all,
We grow strong.
Love may fade,
Pain may invade,
But hope remains.
Believe in you,
See it through,
Sun follows the rain.

In life, we face many challenges. Sometimes, promises we believe in are broken. This can hurt deeply, causing our hearts to ache. But even in those painful moments, we find the strength to keep going. Tears may fall, but they don't last forever. Through every trial, we learn and grow stronger.

There are times when love seems to disappear. It may feel like pain is all around, trying to take over. But amid this darkness, there is always a glimmer of hope. This hope keeps us moving forward, reminding us that better days are ahead. No matter how tough things get, we have the power to overcome.

Believe in yourself. You have the strength to get through anything life throws at you. Even when it feels impossible, trust that you can make it. After every storm, the sun will shine again. Just as the rain gives way to sunshine, your troubles will pass, and brighter days will come.

We all have moments of doubt. There will be days when it feels like the weight of the world; is on our shoulders. But it's important to remember that we are never truly alone. Friends and loved ones are there, to support us, even when things seem bleak. Lean on them when you need to and offer your support in return. Together, we can weather any storm.

Life is a journey filled with ups and downs. Each experience whether good or bad, shapes who we are. Embrace the lessons that come with hardship, and cherish the joy that follows. With each step, we become more resilient, more compassionate and more understanding.

So, when promises break and hearts ache, remember that this too shall pass. Hold on to hope, believe in your strength, and look forward to the sunshine after the rain. You have the power to create a beautiful future, one where joy and peace abound. Keep moving forward, one day at a time, and let hope be your guiding light.

• 51 •

31. Rain

In the gentle caress of rain's embrace,

Shall, it seek to find its destined place?

Longing to be drenched, in your tender hold,

A solitary downpour, in a world so cold.

In tears, I've soaked, in solitude's embrace,

Yet found the strength to seek a new grace.

Was it folly to hope for a fresh start?

To let the rain heal this wounded heart?

Rain, akin to me, in quiet reverie,

In tranquil moments, we find solace, you see.

Together, let us dance in the downpour's embrace,

Rekindling spirits, renewing faith.

Lonely rain, find solace in my plight,

In shared sorrow, find respite tonight.

Though none may grasp the depth of my pain,

In your gentle touch, understanding I gain.

When I depart, let rain be your guide,

To love anew, with someone by your side.

In absence, may rain linger still,

A silent companion, a tender thrill.

Teach us, rain, the art of renewal,

In each droplet, lessons are crucial.

Stay well, dear rain, in your endless roam,

Teach us to live, to love, to atone.

www.ingramcontent.com/pod-product-compliance
Lightning Source LLC
Chambersburg PA
CBHW031509150726
47990CB00007B/2945